W

GROUP Bible resources for 11–14s

Going overboard
Steve Tilley

God's big plan
Jim Overton

1

ALSO IN THE *WORD UP* SERIES:

Get Real with God by Elaine Carr and Emlyn Williams
Pressure Points by Jenny Baker and Phil Wason
The Trouble with Love by John Allan and Steve Bullock
Live it Large by David & Myrtle Lawrence and Lucy Moore
How to be Happy by Terry Clutterham and Jenny Baker

Scripture Union, 207–209 Queensway, Bletchley, Milton Keynes, MK2 2EB, England.
Email: info@scriptureunion.org.uk
Website: www.scriptureunion.org.uk

Scripture Union Australia, Locked Bag 2, Central Coast Business Centre, NSW 2252, Australia.
Website: www.su.org.au

Scripture Union USA,PO Box 987,Valley Forge, PA 19482, USA.
Website:www.scriptureunion.org

Except where otherwise stated, Scriptures quoted from *The Youth Bible*, New Century Version
(Anglicised Edition) copyright © 1993 by Nelson Word Ltd., 501 Nelson Place, P.O. Box
141000, Nashville, TN 37214–1000, USA.

British Library Cataloguing-in-Publication Data
A catalogue record for this book is available from the British Library.

Design: Wild Associates Ltd

Printed and bound by Interprint, Malta.

  Scripture Union is an international movement working with churches in more than 130
countries, providing resources to bring the good news about Jesus Christ to children, young
people and families – and to encourage them to develop spiritually through the Bible and prayer.

As well as our network of volunteers, staff and associates who run holidays, church-based
events and work in schools, we produce a wide range of publications and offer support to those
who use our resources through training programmes.

WHAT'S IN IT

START UP

WORD UP aims to help small groups discover more about living God's way as they read the Bible together. There are two series, with six sessions in each, enough for a 12-week programme. This material can be used as part of a mid-week or Sunday session, at home, at church or in school.

Who it's for

The sessions are written with 11–14s in mind, but older young people might enjoy them too. This book is for whoever is leading the session.

What's in it

Look out for the regular sections to help you plan your time.

Home page:	introduces the theme of each series.
Save as:	aims to help the group think back over what they've learnt from each series and about how they can put it into action.

EACH SESSION

Log on:	ideas to help the group tune in to the session's topic and Bible verses (5 minutes).
Search:	ideas for looking at the session's Bible verses and learning from them (15 minutes).
Download:	ideas for putting what's been learnt into your lives (5 minutes).

OTHER REGULAR SECTIONS ARE:

More:	extra ideas for longer sessions.
Save:	a key Bible verse. You could encourage the group to memorise a key verse each week. See page 62 for ideas.
Help:	extra information.

How to use it

Use the basic outline for a 25-minute session:

1 Log on	(5 minutes)
2 Search	(15 minutes)
3 Download	(5 minutes)

If you have more time, use the extras as described on page 4.

Get ready

1 Pray and read the Bible verses yourself.
2 Read through the outline. Make sure that you understand how the session works.
3 Check for anything you'll need for the session (eg pens, paper) or have to prepare in advance (eg music).
4 Bibles: make sure that everyone will be able to have a copy of the Bible verses that you'll be thinking about, preferably in the same contemporary version.
5 Prepare the place (eg arrange furniture, set up video player) where you will meet, and make sure it's arranged in an appropriate way for the session.
6 Pray for yourself leading the session and for the others in the group.

Go to www.scriptureunion.org.uk/wordup for ready-prepared, simple activity sheets for use with some *Word Up* sessions.

Hear from God every day!

Encourage your group to read the Bible every day with Scripture Union's Bible reading guide for 11–14s – **ONE UP**. For more details, turn to page 64.

5

Going Ov

God said, 'Go east' so Jonah headed west! If you have ever thought about doing the opposite of what God wants then this series of studies is for you. You may not end up as fish puke – but then, Jonah probably didn't expect to either! Got your attention? Good.

Jonah is one of the 'Minor Prophets', the last twelve books of the Old Testament. Don't let that put you off, though. It's one of the best-known books in the whole Bible. It's often forgotten that Jonah's preaching was spectacularly successful. Was he pleased about it? Wait and see.

Try some of the activities on these pages to help your group get into Jonah's story.

Getting into it

1 Find out how much of Jonah's story the group can remember without peeking at a Bible.
2 Now dim the lights, put on some background music and get good readers to read aloud the whole story of Jonah. It's only short.
3 Talk about…
   - What bits had people not remembered?
   - What things and which people could they identify with?
   - Why was this story written down?

> 'I knew that you are a God who is kind and shows mercy.' *Jonah 4:2*
>
> Save

board

Would you do this?

Before you meet, make a list of some tasks of varying degrees of difficulty. Some examples are given below.

1 Give everyone in the group a copy of the task sheet. Ask them to write next to each task how much money they would want to be paid to do it.

2 Talk about the results. What makes a task difficult?

3 Brainstorm. What clues are there that something is what God wants you to do? Write down the group's answers to this and keep the paper until you have finished the series.

Tasks

- Clean all the shoes in your house.
- Get up at 5.00 am for a week and pray.
- Take responsibility for all meals in your household for a month.
- Preach in your church.
- Tell someone who's not a Christian that God loves them.
- Do all your family's ironing for a week.
- Memorise Mark's Gospel.
- Give up chocolate for a year.
- Travel by foot or bicycle only for two months.
- Wash your dad's car.

Go to www.scriptureunion.org.uk/wordup for a downloadable, ready-to-use task sheet.

Sinful cities?

Talk about which cities around the world today have a reputation for sinfulness. Make a list and have a vote to find the 'winner'. What would God want to say to them?

Fish and chips…

Have some fish and chips. When everyone has finished eating, pass round a whole, dead fish, such as a mackerel or trout. Get everyone to feel its oily slipperiness. Welcome to the world of Jonah.

GOING YOUR OWN WAY

 FILE: Bible/Jonah 1:1–3

Reckon you're the only one who is ever disobedient to God? Are you surrounded by super-Christians? Take a at Jonah – even prophets get it wrong!

Log on

1 Bring to the session a few copies of some 'instruction manuals Pass these around and, if possible, include some photocopied from a foreign language manual as well. Ask individuals to say they think the products are and how they are meant to work.

2 Ask the group to think of examples of when they were given s instructions but didn't obey them. What were the consequence

3 Ask if anyone has ever run away from a person or event. What happened?

4 Explain that the story you are going to be looking at together i about a man who had simple instructions to go in one directio but who decided not to follow them.

'The Lord spoke … "Get up and go to the great city of Nineveh and preach against it, because I see the evil things they do."' *Jonah 1:2*

Save

---

board

Help

Nineveh was the capital of Assyria, not a Jewish city. It was in modern-day Iraq but has been in ruins for 2,500 years. Assyria was one of Israel's traditional, and cruellest, enemies. Tarshish was possibly in Spain (experts aren't absolutely sure) but ships that travelled there were always heavy laden and prepared for a long voyage.

Search

1 Have someone read **2 Kings 14:25**. Explain that Jonah, son of Amittai, was a real person, a prophet, mentioned in one of the Bible's key historical books.

2 Now read **Jonah 1:1–3**. Get one person to be the narrator and a second reader to read God's words from verse 2.

3 Use an atlas or globe to show where Jonah *should* have gone and where he actually headed. Explain that God told Jonah to go east to Nineveh, around 1,000 kilometres inland. Instead, he went to the coast and headed in the opposite direction, possibly for Spain, which was 3,000 kilometres west across the Mediterranean.

4 Talk about:

- How do you think you would have felt if God gave you such a huge task?

- Why do you think Jonah ran away?

NEXT

Going Ov

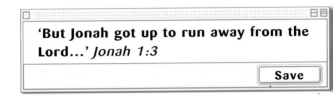

> □ ▦▤
>
> **'But Jonah got up to run away from the Lord...'** *Jonah 1:3*
>
>   **Save**

5 How many different ways can the group think of that the 'word of the Lord' might come to someone (v 1)? For example: visions, dreams, conversations, reading the Bible, adventures, circumstances, voices from heaven. Which of these, or any others suggested by the group, seem the most likely? Comment that we are not told how Jonah 'heard', just that he did.

Download

1 Talk about 'vocation'. Does anyone in the group feel that God is calling them to do something particular now or with the rest of their life? Encourage them and pray for them. Encourage everyone in the group to think about what God might want them to do with their lives.

2 'The Jonah Syndrome' is an expression used to describe anyone who feels a particular call to do something, but very alone in carrying it out. Does anyone in the group need support in a particular solo venture?

3 Pray together for obedience to God when you know he's calling you to do something for him.

Help

The name Jonah means 'dove', which is identified with Israel in the Old Testament and the Holy Spirit in the New Testament.

board

More

On your own?

As an alternative **Log on** activity, get the group to brainstorm people who have a particular talent which they can only carry out alone, no matter how much background support they get (eg individual sports players or entertainment performers: tennis players, athletes, singers, comedians).

Outside the comfort zone?

1 Point out that Nineveh was outside Jonah's comfortable, cultural boundaries – it was a Gentile city as well as a foreign one. Ask the group to give examples of when they've been outside of their 'comfort zones'. How did they feel? How did they cope? Did they feel like running away at any point?

2 What things make you feel comfortable in a situation or place? What are some of your 'comfort zones'? How would the group feel about losing some of them? For example, is life in your church too 'comfortable'? Would making yourselves more vulnerable be a good thing? How could this be done?

No point in running away…

Organise a formal debate, with speakers preparing in advance to speak for or against the motion: 'This house believes there is no point in running away from God.' Allow interventions from the floor, points of order and end with a vote. The chair of the debate should be formal and serious.

Going Ov

CONSEQUENCES

▶ **FILE:** Bible/Jonah 1:4–17

If you run away from God, will you escape? Is it worth the risk?

Log on

- Ask two people to have a conversation with each other, using only questions. The first person to say something that is not a question is eliminated and replaced by a new player. Give a prize to the best questioner.

Or

- Bring in newspaper weather forecasts to read, or video one from TV and play it to the group. Why are we so interested in weather? Brainstorm as many people you can think of who might take an extra special interest in the weather forecast, making sure sailors get a mention.

Search

1 Ask someone to read **Jonah 1:4–17**. As they read the passage, get the rest of the group to provide sound effects.

- Half the group should concentrate on wind and waves, increasing throughout the reading so that the reader almost has to shout by verse 15. At this point, the noise should stop suddenly. Don't allow the noises to peak too soon.

»
NEXT

board

> 'Jonah said ... "I fear the Lord, the God
> of heaven, who made the sea and the
> land."' *Jonah 1:9*

Save

- Others in the group can provide these effects:

  verse 5a: crying and wailing to God, 'Save me' etc;
  verse 5b: snoring;
  verse 7: sounds of dice rolling on a table;
  verse 13: noise, as if people are trying to row, but finding
  it difficult;
  verse 15: fading scream to suggest a man being thrown
  overboard, followed by a splash;
  verse 16: gulps and prayers of frightened sailors;
  verse 17: bigger gulp of a fish swallowing.

2 Refer back to the question game in **Log on**. How did it feel
talking to someone using only questions? What's it like when
someone keeps asking you questions about your behaviour?
Can anyone give examples? Now find the seven questions the
sailors asked Jonah in these verses. There are five in verse 8,
one in verse 10 and one in verse 11.

3 Let everyone make the wind and wave noises again, getting
louder and louder until, on your command, everyone stops
and listens. What can they hear now?

4 Read **verses 15,16** again. Why does the group
think the sailors became more scared once the
wind had stopped?

NEXT

5 What do the verses tell us the Lord did? *(Verse 4: '… sent a great wind on the sea …'; verse 17: '… caused a big fish to swallow Jonah …')*

6 Talk about and compare what Jonah and the sailors believed about God (vs 5–16).

PS We often hear about Jonah and the whale, but what did swallow him (v 17)?

Download

1 Have a time of worship and prayer, focusing on God's power over nature. If it's daylight outside, perhaps you could go outdoors for this. Read **Psalm 8** as part of your prayers. If your group meets after dark you could pray lying on the grass, looking up at the stars.

2 Give everyone an envelope. Ask them to write on the outside: 'God help me to be obedient', and their own name. Give everyone a piece of paper and ask them to write down on it one or two areas in which they know they find it hard to obey God. Tell them to fold the paper, put it in their envelopes and then seal them. Collect them in and promise to give them back at the end of the series.

3 'Throw lots' (eg who draws the shortest straw) to decide which group members must tidy up the room where you're meeting for this session after you've finished!

board

Help

Jesus was so familiar with this Old Testament story that he used it as an illustration of his death and resurrection (Matthew 12:40).

More

Can you throw a double?
Use this as an alternative **Log on** activity. Use two dice and offer a prize to the first person to throw a double. If you want the game to last a bit longer, make it a double six. Make the link with 'throwing lots' (v 7) in the Bible passage.

Good execution!
As an alternative **Search** activity, point out that the sailors couldn't bring themselves to throw Jonah overboard (v 13). Would you have been able to do it? Ask the group how many of them could live with the responsibility of being an executioner.

Going deeper
Read **Mark 4:35–4**, where Jesus calms a storm. Talk about the parallels between this and Jonah's story.

> **'Then they began to fear the Lord very much; they offered a sacrifice to the Lord and made promises to him.'** *Jonah 1:16*
>
> **Save**

HELP – GET ME OUT OF HERE!

▶ **FILE:** Bible/Jonah 2:1–10

Do your prayers need a sense of urgency? There's nothing like being digested to focus the mind! Step forward Jonah and teach us to pray.

Log on

1 Get the group to shout out some understatements. For example: 'It can get a bit chilly in Antarctica'; 'You'd need a couple of goes on a climbing wall before attempting Everest.' Suggest some ones with current interest for your group, for example: '(name of current soccer star) … is OK at free kicks'; '(name of band popular with your group) … are quite a good band.'

2 Don't explain this activity yet. Leave it as a tease.

3 What's the worst place you've ever prayed in? Ask the group to share some descriptions of various horrible places. Point out that none of them will be as unpleasant as the place Jonah prayed in that you're going to read about today.

4 Ask people to tell the group their favourite:
- possession
- place
- person.

Talk about how it might feel to think you've lost them all and will never see them again.

board

Search

1 Read **Jonah 2:1–10** with the sound of running water in the background, for example, leave a tap running or have someone constantly pouring water between two jugs.

2 Remember the understatements from **Log on**. Read **verse 1** again. Is there any doubt that prayer would have been Jonah's first reaction? What else is there to do when you've just been swallowed?!

3 Ask the group to list anything Jonah might have taken on the boat with him. Then talk about what he has now.

4 Get the group to find the bit in Jonah's prayer where he imagines he has already been saved. Read **verses 6 and 7**. Does anyone in the group ever pray like this, imagining how God might answer?

5 Talk together about:
- What's the daftest place you've ever prayed in?
- What would you pray for if you had nothing?
- What does Jonah pray?
- Do you think that people who have been rescued from certain death value life more highly?

6 Point out that God's in charge! He even rules over when and where a fish is sick (v 10)!

'When I was in danger, I called to the Lord, and he answered me...' *Jonah 2:2*

Save

Download

1 Pray positively, thanking God for things he has not yet done.

2 Thank God for all the things you normally take for granted, like Jonah did.

3 Jonah prays, using words possibly recalled from his own worship life (cf vs 2,7 with Psalm 18:6). How much scripture and liturgy can your group recall? Have them pretend to be stranded on an island where they can only encourage themselves spiritually by the things they can remember. (This may be sobering, or encouraging!)

4 Could you memorise together some of the verses under the **Save** headings in this series?

More

Poetry in motion

As an alternative **Log on** activity you could get the group to write some poetry. Get them to think of something disastrous that's happened to them and write a short poem describing what happened. Keep it light! Invite people to share their work. Make the point that the book of Jonah is mainly story, broken up by chapter two, which is poetic in style. You could still make sense of the whole story if chapter 2 verses 2–9 was omitted.

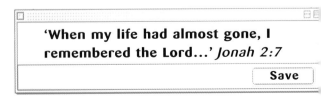

‘When my life had almost gone, I remembered the Lord...’ *Jonah 2:7*

Save

board

Putting it together

Use this as an extra, or alternative, activity for getting to know the Bible passage in **Search**.

1 Type out each verse on a separate piece of paper, omitting the verse numbers. Then add some verses from different passages and some completely spoof 'verses' (eg 'I'm a prophet; get me out of here!')

2 Make enough copies for one each for pairs or threes in your group. Put the sets of verses into envelopes.

3 Read the passage slowly. Then ask the group, working in twos and threes, to assemble the passage like a jigsaw, eliminating the false verses. They must keep their Bibles shut, of course.

Go to www.scriptureunion.org.uk/wordup for a ready-to-use activity sheet.

GO TO

Write a psalm

1 Give everyone a sheet of paper and a pen. Ask everyone to write the first line of a 'psalm' and then pass their paper on.

2 Each person then adds a second line to the new sheet. Encourage people to try to follow the sense and mood of what has already been written.

3 When everyone has got their original piece of paper back, take it in turns to read out the psalms, perhaps with some quiet music playing in the background.

You make me sick!

For a distracting 'time out' have a competition for the person who can do the best impression of a fish vomiting! Have some 'Milk of Magnesia' as a prize.

MIND-CHANGING

 FILE: Bible/Jonah 3:1–10

The shortest sermon in the world ever gets a big reaction. It's ashes and goats-hair underpants time for everyone in Nineveh!

Log on

Before you meet, find out some towns which have a population of around 120,000. Choose one which your group is the most likely to be familiar with.

1 Ask some quiz questions about the place you chose, then make the point that this place is roughly the same size as Nineveh was in Jonah's day.

2 Ask for examples of when anyone in the group has given someone else a second chance. How did it feel to do that? How did things turn out? Today's session is all about a second chance for Jonah (and the Ninevites!).

3 Bring some dominoes to the session. With the group, build them up into a model and demonstrate the 'domino effect', where one domino knocks down the next one and so on. Don't explain why – yet.

4 Comment that when he arrived at last, Jonah didn't say much to the Ninevites (Jonah 3:4), but it had huge consequences!

PS Search the web to find out town populations.

board

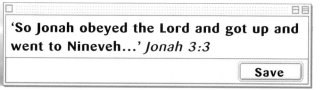

'So Jonah obeyed the Lord and got up and went to Nineveh…' *Jonah 3:3*

Save

Search

1 Read **Jonah 3:1–3**. Now, read again **Jonah 1:1–3**. Ask the group to spot the differences. Why do the group think Jonah changed his mind? *(Possibly this had something to do with being eaten by a fish!)*

2 Read **verse 4**. What short, but very effective, pieces of communication can the group think of (eg 'Fire!')? How many words were there in Jonah's message? *(Seven or eight, depending on the Bible version you're using.)*

3 Read **verses 5–10**. What happened as a result of Jonah's message? Emphasise that God's word is always effective (see also Hebrews 3:12,13).

4 Make a list of the sort of things people do when they are sorry (apologise, pay back, do a good deed etc). What sorts of things did the people of Nineveh do? Why was it important that the king joined in too?

NEXT

Help

Verses 5,6. In Jonah's time, wearing scratchy clothing, fasting and putting ashes on your head were all signs of repentance. Today, on Ash Wednesday, the beginning of Lent, some people still put ashes on their foreheads as a sign of repentance for sin.

5 Read **verse 10**. Refer back to the dominoes. Point out that Jonah obeyed God, delivered God's message and it had big consequences. Make another domino effect to celebrate.

Download

1 Can the group think of any countries where the rulers are apparently unreasonable and evil things are happening? Pray for those leaders and their nations, that there will be change. Pray for any Christians you know about who are living in those situations.

2 Get the group to write letters to MPs, local councils or world leaders about situations they think should be changed.

3 In a time of quiet, invite the group to think about things in thei own lives which they know don't please God. Encourage everyone to ask God to help them put things right and change

More

Doing what God says…

1 Deal out some cards. Give some precise instructions (eg ask players to pick up their cards and, without looking at them, pass any two cards to the player on their left, then look at their remaining cards and put any 3's or 4's face up in front of them).

2 After a few minutes, ask, 'Why are you doing this?' Answers might include: 'We thought it was a game'; 'You told us to.'

NEXT

board

3 Now ask the group to do something silly, which you know they *won't* do (remember safety issues!). Why won't they now obey you?

4 Talk about why we do as we are told. Does it make a difference who told us? Why did Jonah eventually do what God told him?

Rough times

To help you remember the Ninevites' experience, bring in some very scratchy clothes and ask for volunteers to put them on. When they've changed, share some food with the group, but don't give any to those wearing the scratchy clothes. After a while, ask how it feels being left out. Ask the group for ideas about how fasting and wearing uncomfortable clothes is related to repentance.

Prayer walk

Jonah had a long walk to Nineveh, probably over 1,000 kilometres. Take the group on a prayer walk around your area, stopping at various key points to pray.

'When God saw what the people did, that they stopped doing evil, he changed his mind and did not do what he had warned. He did not punish them.' *Jonah 3:10*

Save

Going Ov

ANGRY WITH GOD

 FILE: Bible/Jonah 4:1–4

Jonah tells the people of Nineveh to repent. They do – and Jonah gets cross!

Log on

Try one or two of these activities to get you started.

- Brainstorm things that make people angry. Take a vote on the top three.

- Before you meet prepare a written sign saying (in large letters): 'Make a model of a carthorse'. Give out some modelling clay. Reveal the first three words of the instruction, 'Make a model' and get the group started. After two minutes, reveal the next six letters so the instruction now reads, 'Make a model of a car...' After two further minutes, reveal the whole instruction and let them finish.

  As they are finishing, ask them to share their feelings at your 'changing the rules'!

- Role-play a two-person situation where one actor gets increasingly angry. Perhaps imagine a customer returning faulty goods, or a telephone call to a 'help-desk' which isn't being much help.

Talk about why our anger tends to grow and grow.

board

Search

1 Look at **Jonah 4:1–4**. First, get everyone to read **verse 1** on their own. Ask the group why they think Jonah was angry. Re-cap briefly on chapter 3 if necessary.

2 Read **verses 2, 3**. Have you ever been cross when someone changed their mind? Why was Jonah upset that God saved the people of Nineveh?

3 Refer back to the modelling exercise. Were the rules changed or did everyone merely need to follow the full instructions? Did God 'change the rules' in what he was asking Jonah to do, or did Jonah simply complete his instructions? (Clues in verse 2.)

4 Jonah was so mad with God, what did he ask God to do (v 3)? Can anyone remember when Jonah asked for something similar earlier in the story (see 1:12)?

5 Read God's question to Jonah in verse 4. How many answers can the group come up with? Was Jonah right to be angry?

'Then the Lord said, "Do you think it is right for you to be angry?"' *Jonah 4:4*

Save

Going Ove

1 Who do you think doesn't 'deserve' God's mercy today (eg leaders of evil regimes, convicted criminals, a very unkind person at your school)? Pray together for some of the people you've mentioned. Does anyone *deserve* God's mercy?

2 Jonah prayed, 'I wish I was dead' (v 3). Have any of the group ever felt as depressed as that? Pray for them, being sensitive to people's personal issues. If appropriate, follow these up privately later.

3 Talk about any occasions when people in the group felt angry with God. What happened? Talk about how to keep anger under control, but make the point that telling God exactly how you feel is OK. Is there anything at the moment that the group members feel angry with God about?

More

A God of mercy…

1 Talk about the meaning of the word 'mercy'. What's the difference between 'mercy' and 'justice'? What examples can the group think of? Can mercy *ever* be deserved? Use Nineveh as an example (its punishment might have been justice, but God showed mercy).

2 Give out sheets of A4 paper and some pens. Ask the group to write in the corners the words, one in each: 'justice', 'mercy', 'love', 'repentance'.

3 Talk briefly about the meaning of these words, using a dictionary if necessary.

NEXT

SESSION 5

board

4 To show how these words fit together, tear them apart. Tear the paper once down the middle vertically and once horizontally, so that all the words are now on separate pieces of paper. The gap between the pieces will be the shape of a cross. If you have an overhead projector, use the paper to block out the light; then tear the paper so that a cross-shaped beam of light will be projected.

5 Comment that God has always been a God of justice, mercy and love. This is shown for all time in Jesus' death on the cross, but in the Old Testament, these characteristics of God are seen in his delight at the repentance of evil people.

Help

Read **Jonah 1:3** again. Point out that the verse doesn't say why Jonah ran away. What's the answer in **Jonah 4:2**? Could it be that Jonah had *wanted* to get rid of Israel's enemy?

'I knew that you are a God who is kind and shows mercy. You don't become angry quickly, and you have great love. I knew you would choose not to cause harm.' *Jonah 4:2*

Save

GOD OF MERCY

 FILE: Bible/Jonah 4:5–11

Jonah was angry that God *didn't* destroy 120,000 people and even more angry that he *did* kill a small plant. Welcome to the final part of 'How not to be a very good prophet'!

Log on

1 Bring in a pot plant as a visual aid (either a healthy one or one you've neglected). Ask the group how they would feel if you let the plant die through neglect.

2 Now show them a picture of someone well-known to the group (eg a friend or relative, but check with the person beforehand that they don't mind). Ask the group how they would feel if this person were allowed to die through neglect. What is the difference between the plant and the human being?

3 Ask the group for some examples of times when they've got upset about something trivial. Did they realise their problems were nothing compared to the big problems some people have? Does it help to remember that when you're upset about something? Talk about some of the trivial things we get uptight about.

> 'Jonah ... sat in the shade, waiting to see what would happen to the city.' *Jonah 4:5*

Save

board

Search

1 Read **Jonah 4:5–11**, using three readers: a narrator, Jonah and God.

2 Re-cap on the last two sessions:

- What had Jonah told the people of Nineveh? *(Jonah 3:4 – they would be destroyed in forty days.)*

- How had they reacted? *(Jonah 3:5 – they believed God and repented.)*

- What did God decide to do? *(Jonah 3:10 – he changed his mind about destroying the city.)*

- How did Jonah feel about this? *(Jonah 4:1 – unhappy.)*

3 What point was God making through the death of Jonah's shady plant (v 7)? Does the group think there is any special significance in it being a worm which destroyed the plant (eg worms eat decaying matter and so are a sign of death; eventually, buried bodies will be eaten by worms)?

4 In pairs or threes, role-play some situations in which one person asks lots of pressing questions but the other/s simply walk/s away and sit/s down. Invite people to share their role-plays. Then read again **verses 4 and 5** (God's question and Jonah's walk-out).

5 In pairs or threes, come up with a suggestion for how Jonah might answer the question in **verse 11**. After a couple of minutes, share and talk about your ideas.

Going Ov

Jesus referred to Jonah – 'the sign of Jonah' – several times when he was asked for a miracle to prove who he was. Check out:

- Matthew 12:39–42
- Matthew 16:4
- Luke 11:29–32

Download

1 Give everyone some paper and a pen. Ask them to write a short 'end-of-term' report on Jonah. What sort of a prophet had Jonah been? Was he a good example? Share your 'reports'.

2 Give out the group's envelopes from **Download, Session 2** (page 14). Explain what this is about to anyone who wasn't present at that session. Invite people to share how they have got on in the particular area they wrote down. They don't need to be specific and don't have to say anything if they don't want to.

3 There are loads of people in the Bible, as well as Jonah, who didn't get everything right all the time (eg David committed adultery; Solomon was distracted by many wives; Moses committed murder). Thank God for these people and for the ways God used them, even though they weren't perfect. Pray that God will help you obey him.

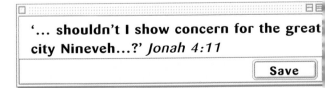

'… shouldn't I show concern for the great city Nineveh…?' *Jonah 4:11*

Save

board

More

People neglect…

Talk about any recent cases of child neglect in the news. Get the group to share how they felt as they learnt more about the story. Emphasise that God doesn't neglect people – but people do.

Pet worms…

If you can, bring in a worm tank, or, if there's one nearby, take people to look at a compost heap. These are great visual aids of life and death. The worms feast on decaying matter and turn it to compost. Make the point that biodegradable means: 'will be eaten by worms and other creatures'!

How do you talk to God?

Talk about the way God and Jonah communicate with each other. Is it like communication between people and God today? What are the similarities and differences?

How selfish are you?

As an alternative **Download** activity, list the following headings: 'Home','School' 'Friends', 'Neighbours', 'Church', or make up others more relevant to your group. Ask each person to mark themselves out of five for selfishness in the way they behave in each of those situations (5 = very selfish; 1 = almost a saint). Get everyone to total up their marks and hand in their score. Now work out your group's average selfishness in each situation and talk about the results. Ask: 'How selfish was Jonah?'

Going Ove

SAVE AS

Cracking story! Rubbish prophet? We've had a fish with a sense of direction, mass repentance following a seven-word message and a king going round in goats-hair underpants. Meanwhile, Jonah cries over the death of a plant, but is not happy at the survival of a city! What had Jonah learnt about obeying God?

Here are some ideas to check you all got the message.

God's will

Look back at your brainstorm paper from **Home Page**, page 7. Having read about Jonah, what new ideas have the group got for how you know what God wants you to do?

The point is…

Ask everyone to try to summarise the book of Jonah in less than fifty words. Share the results.

Decide together what the main point of this story is (eg God loves everyone – even people from Nineveh). Now try reducing Jonah's story to ten words, then five, then one.

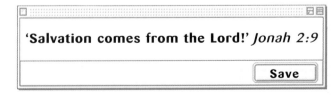

'Salvation comes from the Lord!' *Jonah 2:9*

Save

board

SAVE AS

In the spotlight

In pairs, make up a short drama about Jonah as if 'in the psychiatrist's chair'.

Prophecy now

If God sent a prophet to speak to your village/town/city today what do you think he would say? Would he preach against you or encourage you?

Going overboard for God?

How well did Jonah do?

- How obedient was he? Check out these verses:
  - ▶ Jonah 1:3 – Jonah runs away.
  - ▶ Jonah 4:1,9 – Jonah gets angry.
- How obedient were the people who heard Jonah's message? Check out:
  - ▶ Jonah 1:16 – the sailors repent.
  - ▶ Jonah 3:5 – Nineveh repents.
- Why did Jonah waver between these extremes? Check out:
  - ▶ Jonah 1:12 – sometimes Jonah seemed to accept death.
  - ▶ Jonah 2:6 – sometimes he seemed glad to be alive.
  - ▶ Jonah 4:3,9 – sometimes he seemed to wish that he was dead.

Ask the group:

- How well did Jonah do at going overboard for God?
- Are you doing better than Jonah did?

Help

Some people say this is a story like a parable, and many commentaries on Jonah treat it as being non-historical. Other people believe this really happened. Your group might want to spend some time talking about this, but don't let them get bogged down in the debate. The important thing is what we can learn from Jonah's story.

God's Bi͏g

OK – here's the deal. There's something incredible going on behind the scenes. It might look like everything is normal, but invisibly God is working out his secret plan. The thing is, he wants to let us in on it and become his agents. Are you up for it?

Paul's letter to the Ephesians is all about God's big plan and how we can get involved in the action. Use some of these activities to introduce the series:

Pop profiles 1

1 Say to the group that they're each going to be the subject of an in-depth profile in a celebrity magazine. The magazine needs inside information about what they're really like. Hand each person a blank form and ask them to write entries about themselves for the following categories:

Top tip for life	**Bad habit**
Worst physical feature	**Ideal car**
TV heaven	**Burning ambition**
Hidden talent	**Phobia**

2 Collect them in and read them out in random order. The group should attempt to identify each other from the profiles. What's the main give-away?

N E X

'You were taught to be made new in your hearts, to become a new person ... made to be truly good and holy.'
Ephesians 4:23,24

Save

3 Ask: What describes who you are? Can we get the whole story from what you look like, what you say or what you do?

4 The magazine also plans to interview people who know you. Would they get a different story if they interviewed:

- your mates
- your parents
- your teachers
- God?

Is there someone you'd rather they didn't speak to?!

5 Keep the profiles for use at the end of the series (see page 60).

Go to www.scriptureunion.org.uk/wordup for an activity sheet.

G O T O

Perspective pics

1 Before you meet, take some photos of the place where you meet. Use strange angles, weird close-ups – anything to make the scenes hard to recognise. You might even include strange shots of people.

2 Put the pictures up around the room. Working in pairs, ask the group to identify as many of them as possible.

3 Explain that in Paul's letter to a church in Ephesus we see things from 'God's eye view': what's going on in the world, where it's going, what God thinks of us and what matters most in this life. As God opens our eyes to his master plan, we need to prepare ourselves for some surprises!

THE NEW YOU

 FILE: Bible/Ephesians 1:1–14

Take a good look in the mirror. Notice anything special? Christians might look no different to everybody else, but in spiritual terms everything has changed.

Log on

Use one of these activities to kick things off:

- Carefully remove the label of a can of dog food and wrap it round a can of stewing steak (already cooked!), sealing it with double-sided tape. In full view of the group, open with a tin opener and spoon out some food. Ask someone in the group to take the taste test. (This activity not suitable for veggies!)

  Offer a prize to anyone who successfully takes the challenge.

Or

- Buy three bottles of top brand-name cola drink. Open all the bottles. Fill two with supermarket own-brands. Label the bottles A, B and C. Ask some volunteers to taste each one and to guess which is the real top-brand drink.

  Say that when someone becomes a Christian, you might not notice anything different, as far as you can see. But on the inside an amazing transformation has occurred.

Plan

'He chose us before the world was made
so that we would be his holy people...'
Ephesians 1:4

Save

Search

1 Give several group members the name of a different celebrity concealed in an envelope. Send them out of the room; then invite them to come back in, one at a time, holding the celebrity's name aloft. Tell the rest of the group to act as if the celebrity named had just walked in.

Each time, ask everyone to turn to the person next to them and say, as if very impressed, 'You're in the presence of greatness!'

2 Read **Ephesians 1:1–14**.

Write out the following on a large sheet of paper:

- He chose us to be _____ (v 4).
- He decided to make us his _____ (v 5).
- He _____ us our sins (v 7).
- He _____ his secret purpose (v 9).
- He marked us as his own by giving us the _____ (v 14).

Ask them to find the missing words to give five amazing facts that are true of every Christian. Which of these do you find the most impressive?

NEXT

3 Imagine you could have a 'stars-in-their-eyes' style makeover as a famous person. Who would you be? Imagine it was so convincing people started treating you as if you were that person. What would you do?

Now ask the group to find how many times the phrase 'in Christ' is mentioned in the Bible verses. Draw out the similarities with the above idea. Once we put our trust in Jesus, God treats us as if we were him!

4 Ask: What is God's secret purpose (v 10)? If we know that, how does it help us make sense of life?

Download

1 Bring an old shirt to the session, having tested beforehand that it can be easily marked. Invite everyone to autograph it for you. Talk about what the shirt is worth now. What would it be worth in ten years' time if one of you became famous? Point out that the shirt has been signed by the children of the Creator! Pray as a group, thanking God for each other.

NEXT

'How rich is God's grace, which he has given to us so fully and freely.'
Ephesians 1:7,8

Save

2 Invite everyone to write their address on a postcard, then swap with a friend. Ask the group to write on the postcard some encouraging words, as if from God, from Ephesians 1 (eg 'Did you know I chose you before I made the world!'). Post them in a couple of days' time, so each member of the group receives an encouraging reminder of the session.

More

Body art!

Get everyone to choose one amazing fact about being a Christian from today's verses. In pairs, get everyone to write (in washable pen) on the hand or forearm of their partner a word or two that describes them from God's perspective (eg 'Forgiven', or 'God's property'.)

Secrets

Get everyone to sit in a circle. Each person turns to their neighbour and says:

'My granny's goat guzzles "Wagon Wheels" but she doesn't eat penguins.'

Everyone takes turns to repeat the phrase, guessing what might or might not be on the goat's menu. In each case, tell them if they're right or wrong. The key is, if the word has a double letter, the goat eats it! Keep playing until people spot the secret.

How did it feel being kept in the dark? What was it like when you finally worked it out?

PRAYER POWER

 FILE: Bible/Ephesians 1:15–23; 3:14–21

What's the first thing that enters your mind when you read the word 'prayer'? A heavy chore that you put off? Giving God a list of problems hoping he might hear? In Paul's prayers for the Ephesians, he gives us a glimpse of the amazing possibilities of prayer!

Log on

Roll out a length of wallpaper across the floor. Give every group member a pen. All starting at one end of the paper, ask everyone on a given signal to draw a line, the length of which represents how thankful they would feel towards these people in the following situations:

- a friend who bought you a thoughtful birthday present;
- a teacher who helped you understand a subject and pass the test;
- a friend who supported you through a crisis;
- a surgeon who saved your life.

When Paul heard about what was happening in Ephesus, he couldn't stop thanking God! How excited do group members feel about what God has done for them?

> **'I pray ... that you will know how rich and glorious are the blessings God has promised his holy people.'** *Ephesians 1:18*

Save

Plan

Search

1 Read **Ephesians 1:15–23**. Paul asks God to give his readers wisdom and understanding so that they will know more (vs 17,18). Ask everyone to find at least three things that Paul longs for them to know.

2 Get the group to imagine that they are each going to inherit £100,000 on their 21st birthday.

- How would knowing this change the way they live today?

- If we're looking forward to God's blessings in heaven, what difference might that make to the way we live now?

3 Before you meet, write the word 'Jesus' at the top of a large sheet of paper, then fold it over to hide the word. Ask the group to suggest the name of each of the following, writing them down as you go.

What is the world's most powerful/biggest…

- brand name
- country
- celebrity
- technology
- natural phenomenon?

Ask the group to imagine that one person controls all the things named. Then unfold the paper. Paul says Jesus is greater than all these things (v 22)!

4 Read **Ephesians 3:14–21**. Paul asks God to give his readers power. Find two things that this power can do. What are the limits of this power?

NEXT

5 Comment that God can do absolutely everything. So when we pray for each other, we ought to be as outrageous as our imaginations can muster, praying for the craziest blessings – power, hope and love beyond measure!

Download

1 Roll out another length of wallpaper and have the group line up their pens again. This time, ask the group to imagine that the length of paper represents all the prayers they've ever prayed.

On your signal, ask them to draw lines which, this time, represent how much they pray about…

- health
- school
- worries
- family
- forgiveness.

2 Comment that it's great to pray about everything, but Paul's prayers here are focused especially on the people who already know God – something it's easy to neglect. Use this as an introduction for a prayer time for each other now.

3 Get everyone to write their name on a card and collect them in. Shuffle the cards and deal them out to group members. Invite each person to pray for spiritual blessings for the person named on their card.

4 Challenge them to continue praying for this person in the coming week.

> 'God can do much, much more than anything we can ask or imagine.'
> *Ephesians 3:20*

Save

More

Skydiving!

Before you meet, prepare a list of 'experiences for sale' (eg a trip in a hot-air balloon). You could download these from the Web or find examples in some high street shops. Give everyone a copy of the list, then take it in turns for everyone to choose the 'experience' they think would most suit each person in the group.

Ask everyone to picture themselves doing their dream activity. How might this compare with their feelings about what God has done/will do for them?

Go to www.scriptureunion.org.uk/wordup for a
ready-to-use activity sheet.

G O   T O

Imagine…

Split into threes or fours. Ask them to spend sixty seconds praying, then brainstorm what God might want to do:

- in this country
- in your church or school
- in this group.

Share ideas and then pray about any that catch people's imagination. How might your group begin to make these happen?

Mr Fuller

Give each group of three/four a large outline of a human body. What would someone 'filled with the fullness of God' (3:19) be like? Talk about what God wants us to become, getting everyone to draw on the outline as you do so (eg saying kind words etc). Have each group hold up and interpret their drawing.

WINNERS

▶ **FILE:** Bible/Ephesians 2:1–10

It seems that everywhere you look someone's making a fantastic offer. But often when you read the small print the offer's not all it's cracked up to be. What about God's offer in the gospel message? Is this the real deal?

Log on

1 Before this activity, give one group member a bar of chocolate to hide somewhere on their person! They are to give it, without others noticing, to the third person they speak to in the following activity.

2 Decide with the group on a variation of a handshake. Get everyone to mingle, greeting each other with the group 'handshake' and talk about what they had for breakfast.

3 When everyone's finished 'greeting', ask who got the chocolate. Congratulate the winner in an exaggerated fashion. Interview them about how they feel. Present them with further awards (eg an email declaring that they have won a competition, a certificate).

4 Ask the group why commercial companies often give things away. Do they just want to make us feel good? Does anyone ever give away something for free?

Plan

> 'We were the same as all other people.
> But God's mercy is great, and he loved
> us very much.' *Ephesians 2:3,4*
>
> Save

Search

1 Read **Ephesians 2:1–10**.

2 Draw a line down the middle of a large sheet of paper. Get the group to write:
- in the left-hand column, what the Ephesians were like *before* they were Christians (vs 1–3).
- in the right-hand column, what God has done for them (vs 5–7).

3 Now write 'me' at the top of the left-hand column, and 'in Christ' on the right. Comment that when someone becomes a Christian, it's as if they get a life transplant from Jesus. But how much does it cost?

4 Talk about:
- What made God want to save us (v 4)?
- How did he save us (v 5)?
- What will he show us (v 7)?
- What did we do to earn it (vs 8,9)?

5 Have the statements below (or similar) written out on cards. Get group members to read each one aloud:

'I'm glad I'm not like those selfish brats.'

'I guess I'm just not good enough to be a Christian.'

'God must love me because I'm working with the homeless.'

'Being a Christian is great. You just sit back and let God do everything!'

Challenge the group to spot the attitude problems in each one.

Download

1 Cut out words from magazine adverts that could be used describe how brilliant God's love for us is. Stick them on a wall (with something that won't mark it!). Stand facing the wall together and pray, thanking God for his free gift.

2 Give a card to everyone. Ask them to write on their card the name of someone they know who seems a long way from God. Challenge them to keep the card in their wallet/purse and to pray for them through the coming week.

More

Work of Art

1 Give everyone a square of black card, a metallic pen and some scissors. In pairs, have one person sit side-on to their partner whilst he/she cuts out a silhouette of their face in profile. Then swap places.

2 Read **Ephesians 2:10** aloud together. The first part of this verse could mean that we are God's 'work of art'. Have each person label the silhouette with their partner's name and the words: 'God's masterpiece'.

3 Encourage everyone to write one thing on their silhouette that God has changed in them. On the other side write one thing you want him to change.

NEXT

Plan

4 In the same pairs, or as a whole group, pray about the changes written on the silhouettes, and about the things God might have planned for each person to do.

Transplant auction

Use this idea as an alternative **Log on** activity. If you have a large group, play this in teams, or, for a smaller group, play in pairs or as individuals.

1 Give each team/pair/individual twenty-five coins. Auction to the highest bidder a range of 'items', which are the talents/attributes of particular high-profile people. Add names in place of the descriptions given in brackets below as examples. Include other 'items' for sale that will appeal to your group. Write each 'item' on a card, which is given to the successful bidder for that 'item'. The following are some examples:

- (*A current well-known pop artist's…*) looks
- (*The current prime minister's…*) power
- (*A well-known singer's…*) voice
- (*A famous scientist's…*) brain
- (*A well-known footballer's…*) skill
- (*A very wealthy person's…*) bank balance

2 When all the items have been 'sold' or everyone's spent all their money, talk about: Which team got value for money?

'You have been saved by grace through believing. You did not save yourselves: it was a gift from God.' *Ephesians 2:8*

Save

God's Big

GET WISE!

▶ **FILE:** Bible/Ephesians 4:1–16

**Do you still suck your thumb? Is it time to change?!
When God gives us new life with Jesus, we're like
babies – pretty weak and helpless – but we're not
meant to stay that way. God's plan for us is to help
each other to become strong as we depend on Jesus.**

Log on

Try this quiz. Keep it light-hearted.

1 Who would you hire for a birthday party?
- **a)** The Finley McSmythe Jazz Quartet
- **b)** The Dreggs (thrash metal band)
- **c)** DJ dude and MC cool
- **d)** Coco the Clown

2 What's your idea of the perfect holiday?
- **a)** A coach tour of teashops
- **b)** Topping up the tan on beach
- **c)** Party nights on Clubbers Island
- **d)** A week in Toytown

3 What do you do if you can't get your own way?
- **a)** Go back to doing the crossword
- **b)** Try to discuss the matter sensibly
- **c)** Shout and throw household objects
- **d)** Thrust out the bottom lip and sob uncontrollably

4 What's your idea of comfortable clothing?
- **a)** Tartan slippers
- **b)** Towelling dressing-gown
- **c)** Tracksuit bottoms and T-shirt
- **d)** All-in-one 'Babygro'

NEXT

48

Plan

Scoring

Get everyone to work out their score, as follows:

a) = 4 points; **b)** = 3 points; **c)** = 2 points; **d)** = 0 points.

Add up totals and give everyone the opportunity to share the verdicts:

0–6: Get out of your pram, babe!

7–10: It's that crazy phase, mate!

10–13: A model of maturity, man!

14+: Old before your time, granny!

Search

1. Divide into pairs. Allow two minutes for the pairs to write down everything they have in common. Give a small prize to the pair who've discovered the most. Ask everyone if they think this group is made of people with lots in common.

2. Read **Ephesians 4:1–16**.

3. Have ready a number '1' shape cut out from a large sheet of paper. Place it at the centre of the group and ask them to write on it at least seven reasons from the Bible verses why Christians should work hard at being 'one'.

4. Ask:
   - Does unity between Christians happen automatically (v 3)?
   - What qualities can make togetherness possible (v 2)?

NEXT

'Always be humble, gentle and patient, accepting each other in love.' *Ephesians 4:2*

Save

5 Read again **Ephesians 4:11–16**.
- What are God's gifts for (v 12)?
- What are we aiming for (vs 13,15,16)?
- What are the dangers of not growing up in your faith (v 14)?

6 Verses 14–16. Encourage the group to think about:
- Do you believe everything others tell you about God?
- How do you tell the difference between truth and lies?

Download

1 Think of some 'jobs' which might need to be done regularly in your church, for example:

playing in the music group	**making drinks**
outreach	**setting up and clearing away**
praying	

Add others or delete from this list, as appropriate to your group. Prepare two or three sets of cards on which the 'jobs' are written. Stick them all up on the walls around your meeting room.

2 Explain that each one of these cards represents a way that the members of this group could serve others. Each could be done by more than one person.

3 Put on some music. Encourage everyone to pray on their own for a couple of minutes. Then invite them to come and take from the wall a card which describes a job they'd be happy to do.

4 Read **Ephesians 4:16**. Talk and pray about how you could use your gifts to serve one another.

Plan

More

Body parts

Read **1 Corinthians 12:12–27**. Get everyone to say in less than twenty words what it means to be part of the body of Christ.

Steady on

Give everyone a length of string. Ask them to lay it out on the floor to show the ups and downs of their daily lives and relationship with God. Are there dramatic changes? What could you do to help each other grow steadily in your faith?

True or false?

Use this quiz as an introduction to talking about 'truth' (Ephesians 4:15).

- The Eskimo language has over 100 words for snow. *(F)*
- At least ten people survived, after being in both Hiroshima and Nagasaki when the atomic bombs were dropped. *(T)*
- There is a lake in Massachusetts called Lake Chargoggaggoggmanchaugagoggchaubunagungamaug. *(F)*
- Turtles, once they reach maturity, do not continue to grow old. *(T)*
- You weigh more at the North Pole than you do at the equator. *(T)*

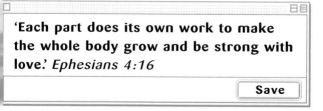

'Each part does its own work to make the whole body grow and be strong with love.' *Ephesians 4:16*

Save

LIGHTEN UP!

▶ **FILE:** Bible/Ephesians 5:1–20

How does God want us to live? Like light, he want us to stand out from the crowd: not greedy, not telling dirty jokes, being wise, loving truth, doing good and being thankful. Does this sound like you? This is what God wants for all his 'holy people'.

Log on

Before the session, collect some items of clothing which suggest what someone is or does, for example:

- an England football shirt
- a crown (make one out of card!)
- a vicar's dog collar
- a local school tie/uniform
- a policeman's helmet

1 Ask members of the group to put these on.

2 Ask the group what they would expect the person wearing each of these to be like/to say/to do. Get the group to stick to your models (use *Post-it* notes) words that describe this kind of person.

3 Ask for some examples of what *wouldn't* look right while wearing the different clothes (eg a policeman committing a crime).

Search

Ask everyone in advance to bring an old, plain T-shirt to this session which won't matter if it gets messed up. Have a few spare ones too, for anyone who doesn't bring one.

1 Get into groups of two or three. Read **Ephesians 5:1–20**. Ask the groups to find out how the Christians in Ephesus are described in each of the following verses:
- verses 1,2
- verses 3,4
- verses 8–12

2 Ask the groups to find out for each description, how Paul said that people like this should live (eg verse 1: God's children/try to be like him). Get the groups to share their findings.

3 Get everyone to draw a T-shirt logo for one or more of these:
- child of God
- God's holy person
- child of the light.

4 Get everyone to attach (or paint) their logo to their T-shirt (use tape, or pins, but be careful!), then put them on.
- What would it be like to wear these T-shirts all day?
- Do you think wearing it would make you behave differently? If so, how?

5 Comment that these logos describe *every* Christian. God doesn't ask us to become his 'holy children' by our own efforts (see Ephesians 1:5; 2:8). The challenge now is to live like we *are*!

NEXT

'Live a life of love just as Christ loved us and gave himself for us...' *Ephesians 5:2*

Save

6 Read **Ephesians 5:6–20** together. Talk about:

- What should Christians avoid?
- What do they need to learn?
- What will help them do that?

Download

1 Talk about: What does this have to do with how we live every day?

2 In pairs/threes, talk about:

- Do you have to go to bed early to be a Christian? (See verse 11; Luke 6:12.)
- Can Christians go to parties where alcohol is served? (See verse 18; John 2:1–3.)
- Should Christians have anything to do with non-Christians? (See 1 Corinthians 5:9–11.)

3 Share your answers.

4 Encourage people to talk about any areas where they find it difficult to live as 'God's children' (eg 'evil' talk and jokes). How could they share God's 'light' with others?

5 Pray for each other.

More

What's your label?

In small groups, ask everyone to count up how many labels they can find on their clothing. Give a prize to the winning group or individual who has most. Are there any labels that they are particularly proud of or embarrassed about? Why do people want, or not want, to wear certain brand labels?

What shows you belong to God? Are you pleased when others notice?

What did you say?

Cut a large sheet of paper into a speech bubble, and draw a line down the middle. In one half of the bubble get group members to write ways we should speak (referring back to this session's passage). In the other half write ways in which we are to avoid speaking.

The bread bin test

Before your session, prepare small containers of foods with distinctive smells, for example: baked beans, parmesan cheese, coffee beans, vinegar, garlic, marmite.

1 Blindfold a volunteer and ask them to identify the smells as you open each container.

2 Talk about:
- Which was the most powerful smell?
- What happens in a room where there's a bad smell?
- What's your favourite smell and why? How does it make you feel?

3 Comment that Jesus' sacrifice is described in today's verses as a 'sweet-smelling' offering to God (Ephesians 5:2). Ask the group to think about their lives as a smell. Encourage them to be honest with themselves. Does it please God, or not? Would they say it's more 'kitchen bin' or 'bread bin'?

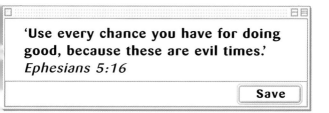

'Use every chance you have for doing good, because these are evil times.'
Ephesians 5:16

Save

God's Big

READY FOR ACTION?

▶ **FILE:** Bible/Ephesians 6:10–20

It's not always easy living everyday for God. Here's some help. Ready for action?

> ### Log on

Have a knock-out contest, using one of these (make sure that no one gets too rough):

- Ask everyone to remove their shoes and socks. (Do this before you explain what they're about to do.) In pairs, get everyone to face each other. Now ask them to lock big toes of their right feet. Conduct a toe wrestling contest – the winner being the first to turn the side of their opponent's foot to the floor. (You might need a generous prize to get them to do this!)

Or

- In pairs, hold an arm-wrestling contest.

Whichever idea you use, the winner in a best-of-three contest advances to the next round. Gather everyone round to watch the final. Award your championship prize.

NEXT

> **'Put on the full armour of God so that you can fight against the devil's evil tricks.'** *Ephesians 6:11*
>
> **Save**

Plan

2 Ask: How easily do you give up in a struggle? In pairs, get everyone to give themselves a 'persistence percentage' in the following challenges:

- fighting over the TV remote
- cycling up a steep hill
- learning a musical instrument
- opening a jam-jar
- understanding maths

Compare results.

3 Comment that the Christian life is a struggle too. Muscles, ammunition, diplomacy or intelligence aren't what's important. In this session you're going to be looking at what you do need for spiritual battles.

Search

1 On a large sheet of paper draw a big square to represent a boxing ring. Label one corner red and the diagonally opposite one blue. Read **Ephesians 6:10–20**.

2 Get the group to write in opposite corners answers to the following questions about the spiritual battle that God's people are involved in, but leave plenty of space in the middle of the 'ring'.

Red corner: Which power is on our side (v 10)?
Blue corner: Who are we fighting (vs 11,12)?
Red corner: What's the aim (v 13)?

3 Get the group to brainstorm situations which might tempt them or be difficult for them as Christians. Have a volunteer write these in blue scattered over the 'ring'.

NEXT

4 Now ask everyone to look in **verses 14–18** for the things that will help them win the 'fight'. Invite a different volunteer to write the group's answers in red amongst the blue writing already in the 'ring'. (*Answers might include: truth, the good news about Jesus, peace, faith, salvation, the Bible, prayer.*)

5 Comment that just as all big fights are backed up by hours of training, Christians need to keep spiritually fit too. Look back at some of the words written in red on your 'ring'. How can we do more to get fit for the fight in some of these areas? For example, talk about how we can get to know the Bible better (v 17) and pray more (v 18).

6 How was prayer helping Paul, the writer of this letter (vs 19,20)?

Download

1 Have card, paper and pens ready. Get the group to cut out shapes from card and paper to represent pieces of the armour mentioned in the Bible verses. Label them accordingly: eg truth, right living, salvation, faith, good news, Bible.

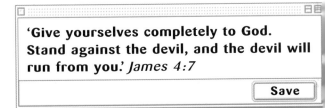

NEXT

'Give yourselves completely to God. Stand against the devil, and the devil will run from you.' *James 4:7*

Save

Plan

> 'Use the shield of faith with which you
> can stop all the burning arrows of the
> Evil One.' *Ephesians 6:16*
>
> **Save**

2 Talk about how the 'armour' might help with some of these:

doubt	persecution	betrayal
fear	illness	poverty
bereavement	family breakdown	failure

3 Comment that suffering and difficulties are a normal part of life in a world which has rejected God. God wants us to 'stand strong' whatever happens. And he's given us some help so that we can do it.

4 Pray for each other and anyone you know outside the group going through a difficult time – that God will give you the strength to keep on standing up for him.

More

Dressed for the job

1 Before you meet, borrow some examples of protective clothing/equipment (eg for beekeeping, ice hockey, skateboarding). Give the group a chance to try some of it on.

2 Talk about:

- How effective do you think the equipment is?
- What are the risks if you forget to wear it?
- Does it still leave any weak areas exposed?

3 Paul stresses that we should put on the 'full armour of God' (v 11). What are the risks if we forget to put some of God's armour on (Ephesians 6:10–18)?

God's Big

Use one of these ideas to encourage the group to take away some lasting reminders about God's big plan.

Pop profiles 2

1 Find the personal profiles that the group members completed at the start of the series (see page 34,35). Hand them out to their authors and give them a moment to re-read them.

2 Ask them to team up with a partner and to fill in a new personal profile, from God's perspective, remembering what you've been looking at in Ephesians.

Date of selection (1:4)
Biggest secret (1:7-9)
Distinguishing marks (1:13)
Strength rating (1:19,20)
Biggest regret (2:2,3)
Favourite present (2:8,9)

Most treasured possession (3:18,19)
Future prospects (3:20)
Occupation (4:12,16)
Relationship to God (5:1)
Role model (5:2)
Top tip for life (5:10)
Arch enemy (6:11)
Habits (6:18)

3 Talk about the differences between the two profiles.

Go to www.scriptureunion.org.uk/wordup for an activity sheet.   G O T O

Christmas every day!

1 Write out the verses printed on the pages of this series (or choose your own from Ephesians). Place each one in its own box with a few sweets. Wrap up the boxes and label each one with a group member's name.

NEXT

2 Give out the wrapped presents to your group members. Before they open them ask: 'What do you like about getting presents?' Ask the group what they can remember from Ephesians about all God has done for us. Why has God given so much to us?

3 Let everyone open their presents. Then ask how they'd feel if they gave someone a present and they…

- just threw it in the bin without opening it
- said a feeble thanks, and walked off
- opened it, but then left it on the shelf for five years
- got really excited and couldn't stop endlessly showing it off?

How should we respond to all God's done for us?

Rapping it up!

1 Talk about what you've learnt about God's big plan from Ephesians.

2 In pairs or threes, get the group to write raps to sum it all up.

3 When they've finished, get each group to teach it to everyone else. Choose one to say together against a backing track.

'In Christ we are set free by the blood of his death, and so we have forgiveness of sins … This was what God wanted, and he planned to do it through Christ.' *Ephesians 1:7,9*

Save

MORE: EXTRA IDEAS

Memorising Bible verses

Save

Try these:

- Set the verse to an unlikely, but familiar, tune. Sing it together.

- Put two sets of individual words from your chosen Bible verse in balloons, then inflate them. Have every person tie an inflated balloon to their left ankle, including the ones containing the words. The teams burst their opponents' balloons to find the words of the verse. First team to find all the words and put them in correct verse order wins. Say the verse together until you've memorised it.

Telling the story

Search

Here are some other ways to help your group into a Bible passage:

- Give everyone in your group a copy of the session's Bible verses. Get them to translate the verses into text message style. Let everyone share their versions. Look out for new perspectives!

- As the verses are read, ask everyone to write three or four attention-grabbing headlines or 'chapter headings' which would give a potential reader a good idea of the content of the verses. Give everyone the opportunity of sharing their ideas with the whole group afterwards.

More ideas in the other *WORD UP* titles.

What next?

If you've enjoyed looking at the Bible together in these sessions, look out for the other *WORD UP* titles each including two series:

How to be happy

- *How to be happy*
  – Terry Clutterham
  … surprising answers from Jesus about the good life.
- *Why suffer?* – Jenny Baker
  … get some help from Job's book.

Also:

Get Real with God by Elaine Carr and Emlyn Williams
Pressure Points by Jenny Baker and Phil Wason
The Trouble with Love by John Allan and Steve Bullock
Live it Large by David & Myrtle Lawrence and Lucy Moore

Each of the two series in each book include six 25-minute group Bible study outlines for leaders. Use them as part of a mid-week or Sunday session, or your school Christian group programme.

Available from Christian bookshops now.
Price: £3.50

Or order online from Scripture Union website:
www.scriptureunion.org.uk

Phone: 08450 706 006
Email enquiries: info@scriptureunion.org.uk
Used this resource? Tell us what you thought!

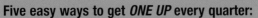